The Brilliant
rty

PLEASE
COME TO MY PARTY!
on Saturday
at 3 o'clock
From Jericho Jones
R.S.V.P.

by Wendy Body

LONGMAN

When Jericho Jones had a party,

Adam the alligator arrived in an ambulance.

He hurt his ankle in an accident.
Where is Jericho Jones?

Bobby the butterfly behaved badly,

BANG!
POP!
Bobby burst my blue balloon!
Have YOU seen Jericho Jones?

and Cathy the cat crashed into the cake.

Careless cat! I'm covered in cake crumbs!

Danielle the dinosaur damaged the door doing her disco dancing,

Oh dear, you've dented the door!
I hope Jericho Jones wasn't behind that door!

and Erica the elephant exercised with eggs.

This is the end of Erica's eggs!

Fiona the foolish fairy fell into the food,

Foolish fairy!
She fell on five fish fingers!
I've seen a flying fairy but where is Jericho Jones?

and Goldilocks giggled as a gaggle of geese got going in a galloping game.

This is a good game!
I wish they'd go and gallop in the garden!

Harvey the horse had Humpty's horrible hairy hat,

Help! He's had my hat!

and Ian the invisible insect slipped in the ink.

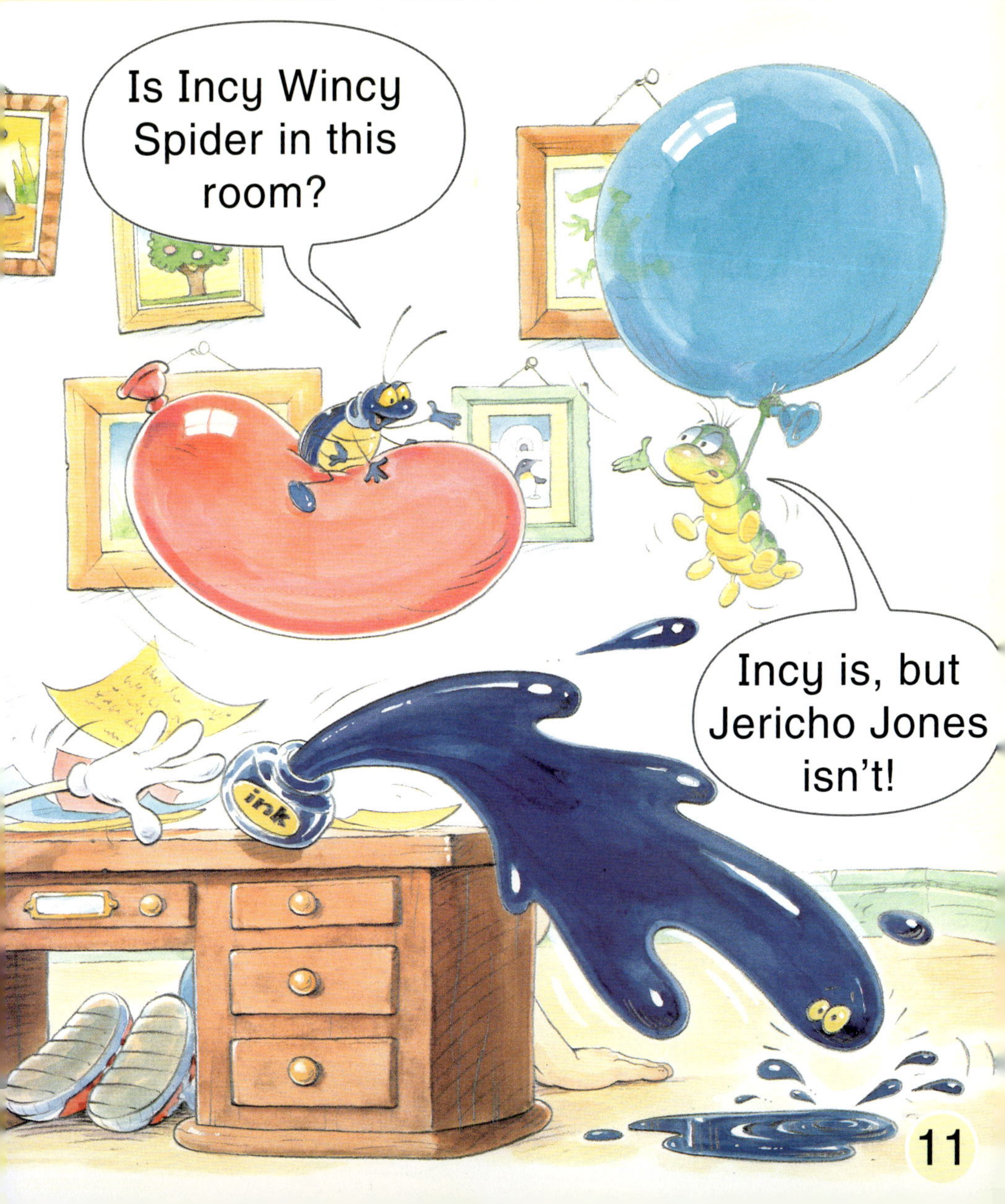
Is Incy Wincy Spider in this room?
Incy is, but Jericho Jones isn't!
ink

Just for a joke, Jack and Jill jumped into the jelly,

Jelly's just the job for jumping in!

and a kangaroo kicked ketchup over Kevin the King.

Jericho Jones keeps his keys in a kettle!
Jericho Jones where are you?

Leo the laughing lion licked a lemon lolly,

What do ladybirds like for lunch?
Loads of lovely lettuce!

and Milly Monster mixed milkshakes and made a mighty mess!

You mustn't make milkshakes with marmalade!
Oh, my mistake ...
Have you messy monsters seen Jericho Jones?

No one noticed Nessie nip off with the noodles and nuts,

I never say no to ninety-nine noodles!

or Ollie the octopus offer the ostrich the otter's orange squash!

I'm off on holiday in October ...
I think Jericho Jones must be on holiday too!

Poppy the penguin pelted the pirates with peanuts, pizza and pudding,

Peter Pirate picked a pickled pepper ...
PICKLES

while the Queen of Quincy quarrelled with the Queen of Quilladoo.

Those queens always quarrel quite quickly.
The question is, why can't I find Jericho Jones?

Rachel the rainbow robot rushed right round the room,

Where IS Jericho Jones?
Sh! I'm reading *The Return of Roger Rabbit* ...
THE RETURN OF ROGER RABBIT

and startled Sammy Squirrel who sat in Spider's spaghetti!

Spaghetti is so soft and squelchy!
Let's sssave sssome sssandwiches for sssupper ...

Tracy the tortoise tickled a tiger till it tipped the teapot over,

Tony and Tina are taking turns to tug the tiger's tail!

and Uncle was unhappy underneath his red umbrella.

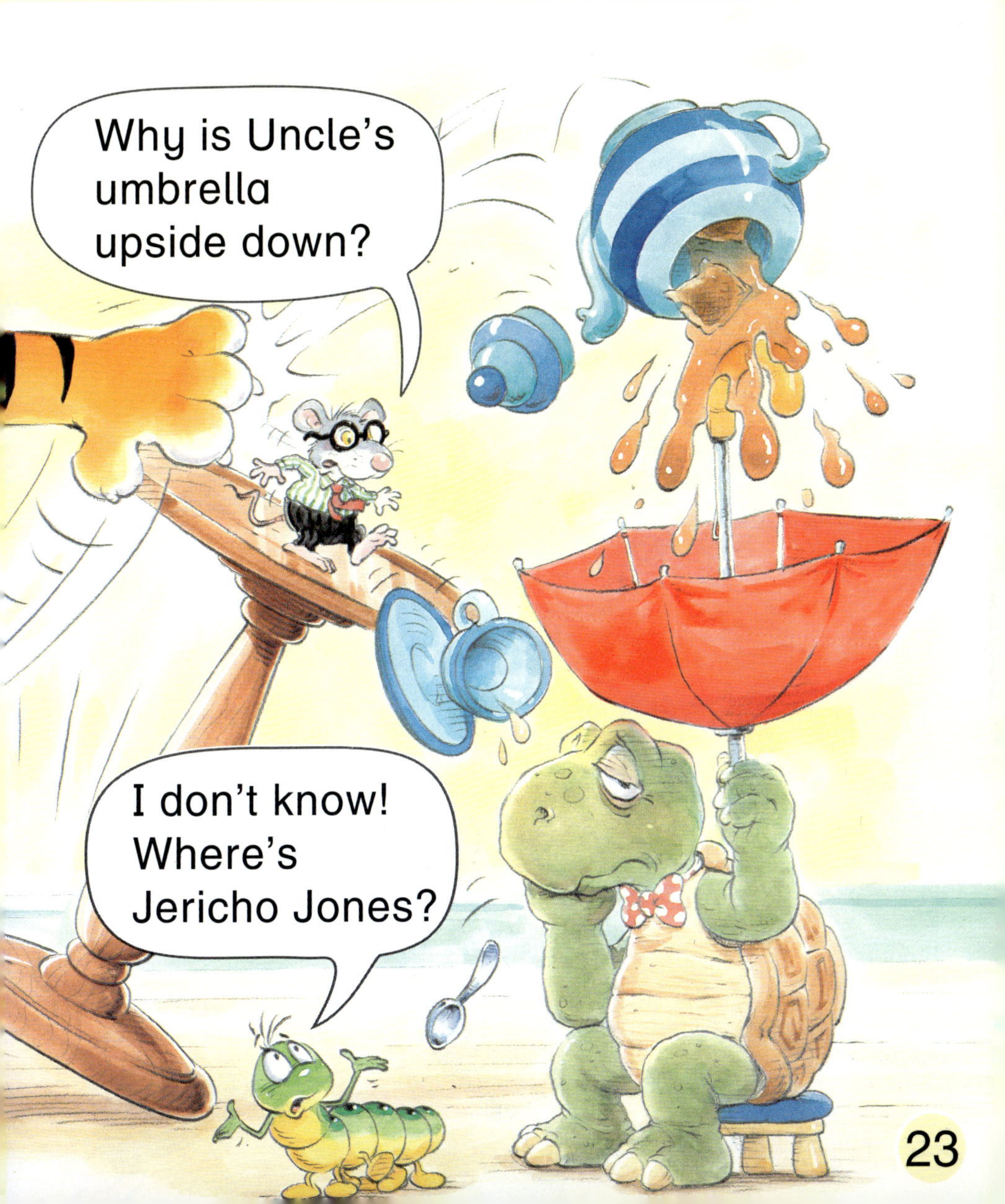

Why is Uncle's umbrella upside down?
I don't know! Where's Jericho Jones?

Victoria the vulture vanished

I love your velvet vest!

when Warren Woodpecker waved a wiggly worm!

CANNED WORM
What a wonderful worm!
I wish I could find Jericho Jones ...

Six foxes had a boxing match,

I'll fix you!
REX
TEXAS IS EXCITING!

and the youngest yelled, "My yo-yo!"

You've got my yellow yo-yo!
Yes – so stop yelling!

The amazing zig-zag zebras zoomed dizzily round until ...

ZOOM
ZOOM
WHIZZ

"STOP!" roared Jericho Jones,

STOP!
Zzzzz

"The party's over

Oh, what a shame!
Things were just getting going!

and it's time to go home ...

Do we have to go?
That's sad!
Where have you BEEN?

but you've got to clean up first!"

I still don't know where he was, do you?